What is this page called?

It is called the endleaf (or endpaper, or in plural sometimes simply referred to as "ends"). Ends are actually four pages (page "one" is glued down, you are looking at pages "two and three" and page "four" is the back of page "three"). Endleaves are necessary to hold your printed pages into the hardcover binding. This book and all *BooksJustBooks.com* children's books have endleaves. They are made of different paper than the rest of the book. These pages may be printed in a single color (most people pick a PMS color) or left blank. They do not generally have any copy printed on them. These pages are not counted into the total page count. Not all books have endleaves. A book without ends is called "self-ended." In a self-ended book, the eight pages of endleaves are counted into the page count. For example, a thirty-two page self-ended book has thirty-two pages out of which eight pages are endleaves and twenty-four pages are the story. In a self-ended book, there is a visible difference in the way the book looks as you open it, too. As you shop around for printing prices it is important that you watch out for whether you are being quoted a "plus endleaves" or "self-ended" product. It makes a BIG difference.

D1383499

endleaf 3

PUBLISHING BASICS FOR CHILDREN'S BOOKS

A Guide for the Small Press and Independent Self-Publisher

Written by Iwana Ritabooke and Ima Bookeprinta

Illustrated by Ikan Coloritte and Marc Tyler Nobleman

RJ Communications, LLC, New York, NY

What is this page called?

This is the title page. This is where you list your title, author, illustrator, publisher, the city of the publisher, and usually your first picture. Children's books are different from other books in that the role of the illustrator may be more important than that of the author. You'll want to keep this in mind as you design this page.

Published by:
RJ Communications, LLC
51 East 42nd Street, Suite 1202
New York, NY 10017

ISBN: 0-9700741-2-3

Printed in Hong Kong

Character Illustrations: Marc Tyler Nobleman
Additional Illustrations: Laura DeSantis, Represented by Leighton & Company
(See Resources, page 33)

Book Design: HSA Design

This is a  book.

Where does the copyright page appear?

The copyright page is almost always found on the back of the title page. We have the copyright notice that includes the word "copyright," the symbol, the year and whoever will hold the copyright. You don't need both the word "copyright" and the symbol. Either will do, but almost every publisher uses both. This is also the place to add any acknowledgements.

Do I have to say in which country the book was printed?

Yes. You not only have to say what country it was printed in, but the size of the type that tells the country of origin (printing) cannot be in a size any smaller than the name of the publisher as it appears on the copyright page. If you do not do this, you could have serious trouble getting your books imported into this country. Also, if you have a jacket, the same "printed in" line must appear on it.

What is this  line?

BooksJustBooks.com will add this to all copyright pages as a symbol of a quality children's book.

Where do I start my story?

This page is where your story starts. In a pinch you could start on the previous page but most stories start on a right-hand page. Now, you're on your own. You have twenty-eight pages left to tell your story and place your illustrations. At the end of your story you will run into the back endleaf. The back endleaf almost always matches the front endleaf. Just like you, we'll start our story here, too.

My name is **IWANA RITABOOKE**. After many long hours of hard work, my friend Ikan Coloritte and I completed writing and illustrating our first children's picture book. We submitted our book to dozens of different publishers with hopes of the book being published. After a long and agonizing wait . . . waiting for the phone to ring. . .waiting for the mailman to deliver an acceptance letter. . .we finally realized that the only way we were going to see our book published was to publish it ourselves.

Soon after the decision to self-publish was made, our luck started to change. After a quick search on the Internet I found and visited *BooksJustBooks.com*. I immediately ordered the free book, *Publishing Basics—A Guide for the Small Press and Independent Self-Publisher*. The first thing we both learned after reading that book was to "watch ourselves." It's a cold world out there. BEWARE of the Vanity Press (subsidy press or whatever they are calling themselves these days). There are plenty of places willing to take your money but few places actually give you value for your dollar. After reading *Publishing Basics* we were left with a good basic knowledge of the printing and publishing process and felt confident to proceed on our own.

Ikan still had many questions concerning the color process because the *Publishing Basics* book dealt primarily with black and white trade books. So we called and spoke to Ima Bookeprinta at *BooksJustBooks.com* and got answers to all of our questions, published our book and now we are in our second printing. Somewhere along the line we decided that it would be great if the three of us would get together and produce another hardcover picture book to present all the questions and answers from our meeting to help other people understand the process of self-publishing. We all hope you enjoy reading *Publishing Basics for Children's Books* as much as Ima, Ikan and I had writing and publishing it.

Hi there! My name is **IKAN COLORITTE**. I am the graphic artist and illustrator. My job is to take the author's words and interpret them into pictures. In a children's picture book the illustrator is just as important as the author so you will find my name on the title page and cover right along with the author's. I'll be asking questions in this book concerning the artwork and color reproduction. If you have additional questions concerning color you can either e-mail me at IkanColoritte@aol.com or contact the folks at *BooksJustBooks.com*.

Hello, My name is **IMA BOOKEPRINTA** and I work at *BooksJustBooks.com*. I have been in the printing business for over thirty years. During that period I have seen many technology changes. The only thing that has remained constant, over the years, is that people love reading printed books and probably always will. I am here to answer questions and help guide you through the printing process. The ultimate goal here at *BooksJustBooks.com* is to help small press and independent self-publishers print quality books while not spending a nickel more than is needed, leaving extra money in the publisher's pocket to promote the book and hopefully come back for a reprint. If you haven't already done so, visit *BooksJustBooks.com* and order a free copy of *Publishing Basics—A Guide for the Small Press and Independent Self-Publisher.* It will help give you a knowledge base before going into the specialty area of children's picture book publishing.

Domestic Printing vs. Printing Overseas
Why can't you print in the USA?

You won't find a more flag-waving American patriot than I but the reality of the situation is that color printing costs significantly more in the US than it does in many foreign countries. Printing prices are made up of two items: labor and materials. Materials (coated paper, plates, ink, etc.) cost pretty much the same worldwide. On a short-run children's picture book, materials make up only about 20-25 percent of the total cost. The rest of the cost is labor. Many countries, especially in the Far East, have significantly lower labor rates than the US. Added to the labor rates are the exchange rates of the various currencies to the US dollar. As quantities rise, and less labor (as a percentage of total cost) is involved per book, the US pricing becomes more attractive. The high-speed web presses and binding lines can compete with pretty much any country on high quantities. *BooksJustBooks.com* currently does all prepress work (scans, proofs, etc.) in the US, but the manufacturing is done in Hong Kong.

If it's so much better overseas, why do most single color books say "Printed in USA"?

The same pricing formula used for color printing applies to black and white printing. The main difference is that the labor/materials ratio is much different. It is not uncommon for a trade paperback book to be 70 percent materials. As a bonus, we produce millions of tons of uncoated book paper in North America so we get a better price in North America for book papers than printers in other countries. Thus, any offshore labor advantage is overcome by the shipping disadvantage.

Can you describe the working conditions in your printing plant?

The primary printer in this program is headquartered in Hong Kong with a staff of more than 700 employees coordinating the printing and binding of more than 20 million books annually. All employees are at least 19 years old and are employed under yearly contract which guarantees maximum daily and weekly hours, as well as room and board and four daily tea/lunch breaks. Many employees are in their fourth or fifth yearly contracts.

Our manufacturers are creating satisfactory work environments in China—a country where there are more jobs than there are qualified people to fill them. Any *BooksJustBooks.com* customer is welcome to tour any of our facilities at any time.

BooksJustBooks.com offers single color books in quantities as low as 100 copies.

Why can't I print fewer than 1000 copies of my full-color book?

Short run digital technology for black and white printing has been around for quite some time now. The original "docutech" technology was designed for one purpose: to produce short run black and white books economically. On the other hand, while there have been digital color presses on the market for some time now, their original intent was more of a commercial nature like ad sheets, postcards, etc. and not book printing. Thus the "per impression" cost is OK for single sheet items, but it is very cost restrictive for multi-page items like books. Digital presses are now in widespread use for printing book covers but a cover is a single sheet item. Eventually you will probably be able to run short run color books economically but not now. All books in the *BooksJustBooks.com* children's book program are printed on traditional sheetfed printing presses.

I know that paperback binding is less expensive. Why doesn't _BooksJustBooks.com_ offer paperback pricing for children's picture books?

No matter how good your book is, you cannot sell your book for a price much higher than the current "market" price. The stores/consumers could care less what you paid to print the book. They only care what the retail price of the book is as compared to other books in the category. Large publishers sell a 32-page paperback color children's book for as low as $1.29 and never higher than three or four dollars. In order to retail books for that price the publisher needs to be able to buy them from the printer for between twenty-five cents and seventy-five cents each. How do they do that? They print 50,000 to 100,000 copies at a time and usually group four to six different titles at a time

for a total of 200,000 to 600,000 books. The truth is, you are not going to print in these quantities so you are not going to get these printing prices so you are not going to be able to sell at the same retail price. In short...you can't compete. Hard-cover books are different. Even the large publishers print much lower quantities of hard-cover books. The result is that their printing costs are higher and their retail costs are higher. Add to this that the large publishers have much higher fixed costs and the result is that you, as a small press publisher, can compete with the large publishers by only buying 1,000 copies and up.

What types of originals are used for illustrations?

Illustrations can either be original artwork, photographs, transparencies (35mm and larger), computer generated graphics (in Illustrator, Photoshop, etc.), digital photos (photos taken with a digital camera) or photo CDs (traditional film scanned to CD at time of processing). Keep in mind that original art must be bendable and the largest size that can be efficiently handled is 12" x 18". Art any larger than that needs to have a transparency made, or, be scanned on the more expensive drum scanner. Note that in making a transparency you are a generation away from your original from a quality standpoint, but the cost can run several hundred dollars per transparency which could ruin the budget on a 32-page book. So, in either case, large artwork costs you more.

Is there one medium that's better than another?

No, not really, but keep in mind that scanners "see" everything. So if you have layers of watercolor, or if you erased anything, those things will get picked up. If you are in doubt about how your artwork will scan, we suggest you send us an image to test.

What size should my original art be?

Always keep in mind the trim size of your book and work proportionally with that size. In other words, if your book is going to be an 8" x 8" (square) book, the artwork should be square. If it isn't, when you reduce or enlarge your artwork, something will be lost in order to have what you use be square. Also, ALWAYS ALLOW FOR BLEED if you indeed want the illustrations to bleed. Bleed is when your color goes to the edge of the book. In order to do that, the printer needs a minimum of ⅛" "extra art" at each edge. So, don't have a character's head at the edge of your artwork unless you intend to crop the head on the page.

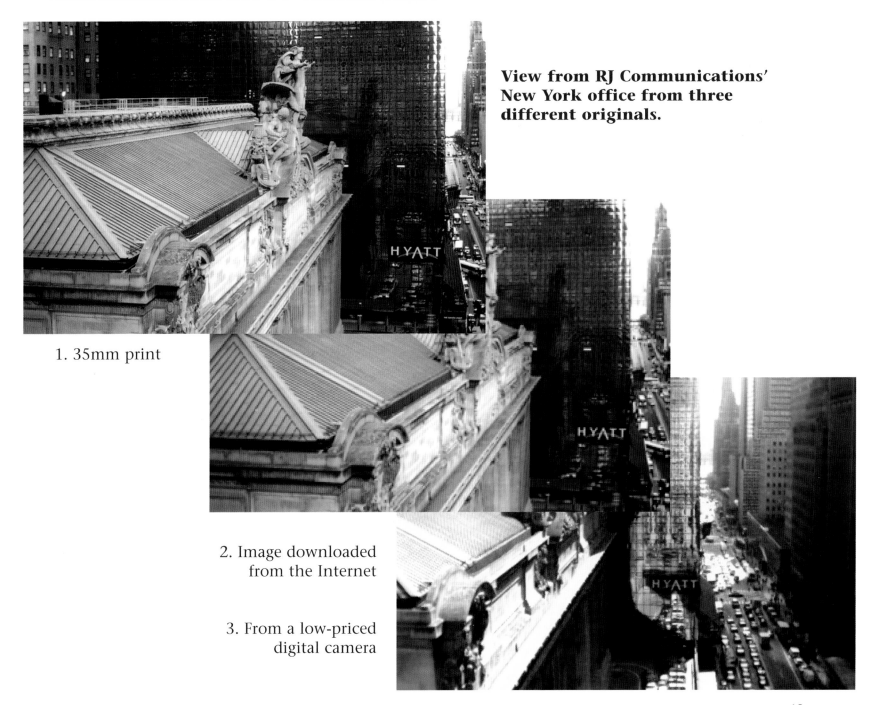

**View from RJ Communications'
New York office from three
different originals.**

1. 35mm print

2. Image downloaded
from the Internet

3. From a low-priced
digital camera

1. Commerical scan

2. Average consumer scan

What is a scan?

Simply put, a scan takes a continuous tone picture and separates it into dots that a press can print from. These dots are not always visible to the naked eye. All scanners are capable of producing adequate scans for use on the Internet. Very few scanners used by the average consumer are capable of producing a scan that can be used for quality printing.

Should I provide my own scans?

NO! It's as simple as that.

Can I supply my own scans and save money?

No. Very few people have a scanner that will produce an acceptable product for print reproduction. We have shown examples throughout this book of a variety of originals scanned on various quality scanners. More than 99.9 percent of the quality problems that occur are the result of customer supplied scans.

The *BooksJustBooks.com* children's picture book program is priced so aggressively that even with including the scans *BooksJustBooks.com* is less expensive than almost any printer in the world, especially for runs of 1,000 copies and up.

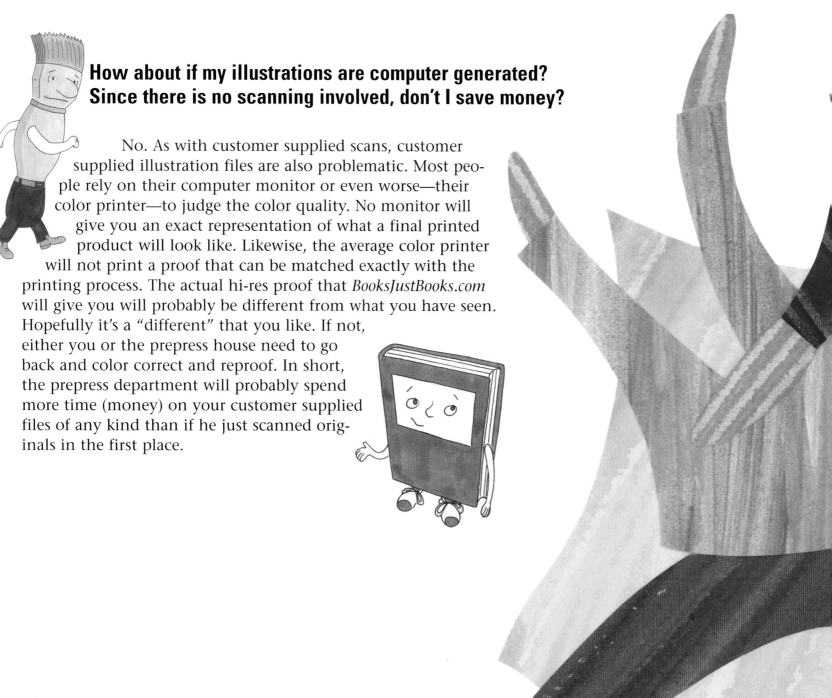

How about if my illustrations are computer generated? Since there is no scanning involved, don't I save money?

No. As with customer supplied scans, customer supplied illustration files are also problematic. Most people rely on their computer monitor or even worse—their color printer—to judge the color quality. No monitor will give you an exact representation of what a final printed product will look like. Likewise, the average color printer will not print a proof that can be matched exactly with the printing process. The actual hi-res proof that *BooksJustBooks.com* will give you will probably be different from what you have seen. Hopefully it's a "different" that you like. If not, either you or the prepress house need to go back and color correct and reproof. In short, the prepress department will probably spend more time (money) on your customer supplied files of any kind than if he just scanned originals in the first place.

19

How do I prepare my text?

Text and art are two different things. Text typically prints in black (and black only, not black made up of four-colors). And art typically prints in four-color. So, when creating your artwork remember to leave space where your text is going to be placed. This can be either an area with no artwork or an area that is light in color, and an area that is not too busy. Remember, you want to be able to read your type, and that won't be possible if type is in with your artwork. When creating your digital files, do not combine the art and the text. The text should always be a separate element.

In order for your text to be "understood" by *BooksJustBooks.com*, it needs to be in either Quark or Pagemaker. You will need to have lo-res scans in your files too to indicate where your artwork is to be placed. If you do not have a scanner, that's OK too, because *BooksJustBooks.com* can provide you with lo-res scans for you to place.

What kind of proofs will I see?

The first proofs you see will be Iris proofs. These proofs will be either of the illustrations only (if *BooksJustBooks.com* does the scans) or full pages with text if electronic files are supplied. These proofs are the proofs that will be followed at the printing press. If the proof has a red cast, the final printed product will have a red cast. No proof, however, is 100 percent. The Iris is about 90 percent of what you'll see on the printed product. (Note: In my experience most artwork tends to get richer/darker.) Without getting too technical, let it suffice to say that exact match proofs are only provided to publishers who have exact match budgets. After the Iris proofs are OK'd a final book proof will be supplied. This final proof is not meant for color OK. The pressman uses the OK'd Iris proofs. This final proof is meant to make sure that page one is in front of page two and that all type and graphic elements are in their proper places.

Are you saying that the printer will not match my artwork exactly?

Yes. Always keep in mind that, only you, your designer and possibly your brother, sister, mother or grandmother have actually seen your original artwork. It's sort of like the "tree falling in the woods" thing. If your color is not exact, will anybody know? The printer will print a reasonable match. If you cannot live with 90 percent . . . STOP NOW! Read no further. Unless you are independently wealthy and do not mind spending a sizable portion of that wealth on book printing, you should not attempt to self publish. Save your money. You are only going to drive yourself crazy and even worse than driving yourself crazy, which is your right, you will drive the poor printer crazy, too. Life is too short. Pick something else to do with your money.

What's all this FOB, CIF, DDP stuff I read on printer's quotations under shipping?

FOB stands for **Free On Board** to a particular port. US printers quote FOB most often, but when used internationally it means that the printing price only covers delivering your finished books to the ship's rail ("on board") at the named port of shipment. The cost of delivery, and insurance to your location is totally your responsibility.

CIF is an abbreviation for **Cost, Insurance, and Freight** to a particular port. Not all US ports are actually cities that you can sail a ship to. This helps people who do not live on a coast. There are 32 ports—they are:

Atlanta, GA	Minneapolis, MN
Baltimore, MD	Nashville, TN
Boston, MA	New Orleans, LA
Buffalo, NY	New York, NY
Charleston, SC	Norfolk, VA
Charlotte, NC	Philadelphia, PA
Chicago, IL	Phoenix, AZ
Cincinnati, OH	Pittsburgh, PA
Cleveland, OH	Reno, NV
Dallas, TX	Salt Lake City, UT
Denver, CO	San Diego, CA
El Paso, TX	San Francisco, CA
Houston, TX	Savannah, GA
Los Angeles, CA	Seattle, WA
Memphis, TN	St. Louis, MO
Miami, FL	Tampa, FL

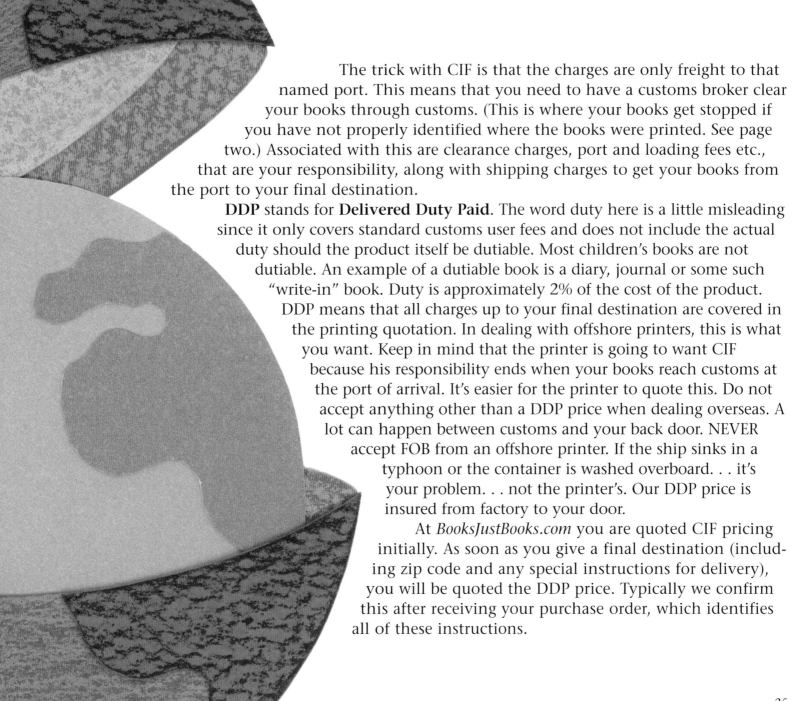

The trick with CIF is that the charges are only freight to that named port. This means that you need to have a customs broker clear your books through customs. (This is where your books get stopped if you have not properly identified where the books were printed. See page two.) Associated with this are clearance charges, port and loading fees etc., that are your responsibility, along with shipping charges to get your books from the port to your final destination.

DDP stands for **Delivered Duty Paid**. The word duty here is a little misleading since it only covers standard customs user fees and does not include the actual duty should the product itself be dutiable. Most children's books are not dutiable. An example of a dutiable book is a diary, journal or some such "write-in" book. Duty is approximately 2% of the cost of the product. DDP means that all charges up to your final destination are covered in the printing quotation. In dealing with offshore printers, this is what you want. Keep in mind that the printer is going to want CIF because his responsibility ends when your books reach customs at the port of arrival. It's easier for the printer to quote this. Do not accept anything other than a DDP price when dealing overseas. A lot can happen between customs and your back door. NEVER accept FOB from an offshore printer. If the ship sinks in a typhoon or the container is washed overboard. . . it's your problem. . . not the printer's. Our DDP price is insured from factory to your door.

At *BooksJustBooks.com* you are quoted CIF pricing initially. As soon as you give a final destination (including zip code and any special instructions for delivery), you will be quoted the DDP price. Typically we confirm this after receiving your purchase order, which identifies all of these instructions.

What costs are not included in the *BooksJustBooks.com* estimate?

Your "prepress" is done in this country and your books will be manufactured in Hong Kong. *BooksJustBooks.com* takes care of sending your original artwork to the prepress plant and delivering the material to the plant in Hong Kong. It is your responsibility to return any proofs to the prepress plant. Also, the prices are quoted CIF to a US port. The additional cost for a DDP delivery is yours. See page 24 for the explanation of this.

What can I expect in terms of timing and schedule?

Count on receiving books in ten to twelve weeks from when you deliver your material to *BooksJustBooks.com*.

Here are the steps and the time involved for a typical book:

- Job is received in New York and sent to prepress plant.
- Proofs of the artwork are delivered to you approximately one week and two days later.
- You review the proofs and return them to the prepress plant—this could be one day or two weeks, it's up to you!
- Upon receipt of your proofs, if the color is OK'd, or has minor corrections, prepress will make the changes and place your scans in your text document and generate a set of proofs. You can expect to receive these in a week.
- Again, the timing on the review of your proofs is up to you.
- Upon receipt of OK'd proofs, material for the printer is received in New York in three days.
- Hong Kong receives that in another day or so.
- Hong Kong will send you one final proof to OK. This proof is not for color. This serves as a final check that all elements are in their correct place. Any editorial changes at this point are quite costly. You do not need to send this back, simply fax us and let us know we may proceed. Assuming this all happens in a timely manner, your books will take four weeks to manufacture.
- When books are ready, we send you one advance copy followed by a final invoice.
- This invoice is due prior to delivery (which is typically three weeks from this date).
- Arrival notice of books will be given to you either by e-mail, fax or phone. Often you will need to discuss the actual delivery details with the local company who is making the delivery.

What do I do when, "I am ready to go to press"?

Send your purchase order, original art and payment to *BooksJustBooks.com*. You create the purchase order at the website and it is very important that all of the information we request be provided, particularly the shipping address and all delivery instructions. Once we have your actual PO, we will figure the DDP price (see page 24 for more on this) and if any details are incorrect that could affect not only the price but also the actual delivery of your books. (For instance, we need to know if your address is residential and if we are to deliver to a garage, second floor, etc.)

When my book sells out, does a reprint cost less than the first printing?

Yes. The amount of savings depends on several factors. Contact *BooksJustBooks.com* for details.

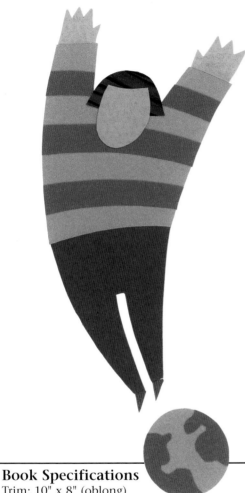

Resource List

General Web Sites
Copyright Office — http://lcweb.loc.gov/copyright (Library of Congress)
ISBN — www.bowker.com/standards/home/isbn/us (RR Bowker)
Book Design — www.rjcom.com/hsa.cfm (HSA Design)
Editorial Services — Kathy O' Hehir – Bookartisan@aol.com
Distribution — Amazon.com- www.amazon.com (Advantage Program)

Illustrators
Children's Illustrator Directory — www.inkspot.com/illus
Leighton & Company — www.leightonreps.com
Marc Tyler Nobleman — http://www.mtncartoons.com/

Newsletters
Children's Book Insider — www.write4kids.com

Trade Associations & Organizations
Children's Book Council — www.cbcbooks.org
Poets and Writers Online — www.pw.org
Small Press Center — http://smallpress.org/
Society of Children's Book Writers & Illustrators' — www.scbwi.org
SPAWN (Small Publishers, Artists & Writers Network) — http://spawn.org

Book Reviewers
Bloomsbury Review — http://bookforum.com/bloomsbury/
ForeWord Magazine — www.forewordmagazine.com
Independent Publisher — www.bookpublishing.com
Library Talk — www.linworth.com

RJ Communications
51 East 42nd Street, Suite 1202, New York, NY 10017
Phone: 800-621-2556   Fax: 212-681-8002
customerservice@rjc-llc.com
West Coast Office: Phone: 800-754-7089 Fax: 310-318-6235
rjcwest@msn.com

Book Specifications
Trim: 10" x 8" (oblong)
Pages: 32 plus ends plus case
        with printed casewrap
Text: Printed 4/4 on 128 gsm matte
Endpapers: Printed 1 (PMS)/0
        on 140 gsm woodfree
Casewrap: Printed 4 plus film lamination/0
        on 157 gsm gloss
Binding: Smyth sewn flatback
        with 3mm boards